MW01488909

I'm Coming Out of This

BEVERLY ANN SMITH-GLASPER

ISBN 978-1-0980-1254-0 (paperback)
ISBN 978-1-0980-1255-7 (digital)

Copyright © 2019 by Beverly Ann Smith-Glasper

All rights reserved. No part of this publication may be reproduced, distributed, or transmitted in any form or by any means, including photocopying, recording, or other electronic or mechanical methods without the prior written permission of the publisher. For permission requests, solicit the publisher via the address below.

Christian Faith Publishing, Inc.
832 Park Avenue
Meadville, PA 16335
www.christianfaithpublishing.com

Printed in the United States of America

ACKNOWLEDGMENTS

First giving honor to God who is the head of my life and the author and finisher of my faith.

I would like to thank all those who made it possible for me to be here and be who I am today. I want to thank you all for the PUSH, which are the "pray until something happens" moments in my life. I'm so grateful to all of you.

First giving honor to my mother, Anita Louise White; my great-grandmother, Mary L. Grandberry; my great-great-grandmother, Jenny McCrary; and most of all, Beverly M. Clerkley, my grandmother, she thought enough to raise me in the fear and admonition of the Lord.

To my loving pastor, Illona W Dickson, I love you every day.

I would like to credit Angela Sinkfield for her believing in me and working so hard to put my words in a notebook into a book form. The creation of my life as a living epistle for those who need help and struggle with what I have been delivered from in my life. Lisa McKnight, thank you for your expertise. To my big sister, Kia Jeffrey and Aretha Patterson. Special thanks to James and Vanteen Bailey.

And last but never least to my king and my partner for life, Charles Glasper Jr. Oh, I have found the one whom my soul loves forever.

Love always,
Beverly Ann Smith-Glasper

C H A P T E R   1

And What You Won't Do...
Someone Else Will!

Who walked on water? Peter! Okay, who was in prison, two men? Paul and Silas! Good. The Jehovah Shammah Church of God is leading by forty points. Quickly, recite the passage of John the Revelator's experience for the winning points please. All right, Shawnta, your hand was first representing Jehovah Shammah Church of God. "I John was on an aisle called Patmos. I was out there for the word of God and the testimonies of Jesus Christ." The winner of our Council Bible Bowl is the Jehovah Shammah Church of God. God bless you all and keep up the good work.

Suddenly, in the sanctuary where I witnessed the glory, entered a nice, buffed hunk of a man who approached me after service and said, "Praise the Lord, how are you!"

I replied, "Well, praise Jesus, I'm fine and yourself?"

He said, "That was some good knowledge you gave on your side. My name is Jaquis, what's your name?"

I said very quietly, "Shawnta."

He said, with a sigh in his breath, "Um, so will you be here tonight?"

I looked at him like, are you kidding me? We are the host church for the Council and our church just won the Bible Bowl. I said sarcastically, "No, uh, uh. I above all want to be here. Will you be here is the question?"

He said, "Yeah, I live just around the corner on Spectrum Avenue."

"Oh, yeah." I replied. "I live on Prosper Avenue one block over. But I'm leaving until this afternoon. We're serving lunch downstairs and my bishop would like me to serve the Bishop's Table only."

"Well, you must be someone special to do that task."

"I don't think so, Jaquis, I'm just the Bishop's goddaughter, and he feels I have a spirit of servitude."

"You know what?"

"Yes," I said.

"I will stay for lunch and join you, if you don't mind?"

I then exclaimed, "Okay!"

Later on, lunch came and went.

"And now I must change for church tonight, Jaquis. Thanks for keeping me company."

"Hey, how are you getting home?" he asked.

I said, "Well, I'm walking, what about you?"

He said, "I'm walking as well."

"So, Jaquis, will you walk me home?"

He said, "Sure!"

We walked and talked until we came upon a huge puddle, in which I couldn't get across without getting my shoes and feet really wet. So he picked me up and carried me over the puddle. I said to myself, *He's such a gentleman and he's strong and sexy too.* I felt like I had just entered dreamland. I was really a queen and my king had finally come. There was only one small problem: I was fifteen and he was nineteen. As it goes, the old saying was, *age is nothing but a number.* Yeah, but in this case, a statutory rape number plus an older teen age guy equals perverted prison time. I decided we would just be friends.

So about two months had passed and he would meet me at my school bus stop and walk me home. Jaquis had one sister who I took a liking to because we all played basketball, softball, kickball, raced, and jumped fences like someone was after us. Until one day I got really brave. I saw Jaquis's dad, the good Reverend Allen Hopewell. I said to him, "Hi Mr. H."

He said, "Hey, babe, how are you doing."

"Fine, sir," I replied. I spoke to him a few minutes and then replied, "Sir, I really like your son, do you mind if I date him?"

He called for Jaquis, "Hey, boy. Get your butt out here!"

Jaquis, standing inside looking out of the screen door, says, "Sir."

"Hey, man, this is going to be your wife if you let her get grown. She has asked permission to date you."

Jaquis started laughing like Popeye as he always has done. I was trying to look somewhat serious, but just hearing Jaquis laugh would make anyone laugh.

So we went on for about two years dating and liking one another. I went to my Grandma Marcellena's house one weekend; she raised me in place of my mom. However, I lived with my great-great grandma Genine Pointer. She was getting quite up in age and I loved her dearly. So I went to help my Aunt Delilah take care of her mom as well as go to school from her house. Jaquis and I had a wonderful relationship going until my Grandma Marcellena found out, and she said, "That young man is too old for you and you must stop seeing him immediately. There is no dating or boyfriends until the appropriate time."

Then to make sure I didn't see him, she called Rev. Hopewell to talk to him about Jaquis. So Jaquis went on and I did as well.

Although we talked at church functions and on the telephone, it still wasn't the same. Then out of the blue, Jaquis came over to my church and was sitting in the rear. He met a young lady by the name of Stacey. She was too hot to trot. He asked her as he saw me directing the choir, "Who is that young lady?" He couldn't see my face and he said, "She's really good at that."

Stacey said, "Um, huh! You don't want to know her, she thinks she's holier than thou."

So when service was over, I went over to speak to him. He paused and said, "That was you, Shawnta? You never told me you direct like that or even that you were a director at all for that matter."

I told him, "The Bible says, "Boast not in yourself, right?"

"I guess you're right."

"Well, I see you've embarked upon Miss Thang," I said sarcastically.

He said, "Who, Stacey?"

I said, "Oh Lord, forgive him for he knows not what he has done. He knows her name and that's enough to send him to hell, Lord."

I've always made funny statements that no one has ever thought to say or put together. This was my little form of humor. So I asked Jaquis how he was doing and all, and I found out later he was talking to Stacey. Then, he made a mistake and called me her name. I told him, "If you want to be caught up with her, then so be it. A saved young lady not putting out sex is not who you want. You want a fully developed girl to lie to you and get as many phone numbers in a month's time as she can. Well, Jaquis, I'll talk to you later."

Then, after a few months of chatter, summer had come and I still spoke to him on the telephone. Then I met a boy my age who went to the Pentecostal Place of Salvation Church. His pastor was a female, the late Pastor Jones. His name was Royale. We liked each other a lot. We were in the WWDC (World Wide District Council) together. When we met, I was now 16½, ready for my Junior Ring Dance.

Well, Royale ask to take me and I said, "Okay."

Well, the night had finally come and Royale never showed up. I waited two hours for him to arrive. Then my grandmother said, "Call Jaquis."

I said, "What!"

I rushed to the phone like the mighty rushing wind on the day of Pentecost. I asked to speak to Jaquis almost in an unknown tongue because I was so excited. The telephone rang and rang. Then I started praying, "Lord, let him answer, let him pick up, let him pick up"—see I told you, I almost spoke in tongues. I was happy he answered. He said, "Hello."

I said, "Ah, Ah, Jaquis," I just screamed. I couldn't talk. I said, "Hold on."

I gave the phone to my grandma Marcelina. She said, "Listen, Jaquis, I know I'm the one who said you all can't see each other, but I have spent good money on this dress and she's not going to Junior Ring Dance alone. And besides, she's too pretty and I was wondering would you escort her to the dance."

Jaquis said, "Sure. I'll get dressed and I'll be right over."

Thirty to forty minutes passed and in walked this nice, suave-looking, muscle-bound dude with a bald fade and muscles everywhere. God put this together fabulously. Even down to our clothes. I wore a velvet/white satin dress with white satin puffed short-sleeve arms and a satin bow that wrapped around the breast and tied in a bow in the back and the bow had layers on it. From the torso to the knee was black velvet. Jaquis had on white tux pants with a black short V-neck lapel with black shoes. We were sharper than two tacks holding up the finest tapestry curtains.

Well, as the seasons change, people change, so we kind of drifted apart after that episode in our lives. Jaquis and I would see each other periodically once again at church conferences, revivals, and seminars. As I grew up and went on in the Lord, I was called into the ministry at age fifteen, but I didn't accept my calling until I was seventeen years old. This was the highest point of my life. At the same time, there was a young man who was assigned to me. I mean assigned by the adversary as a distraction. Assigned as a distraction so that I wouldn't make my calling an election sure. But as much as I tried to put him out of my mind, I was in a spiritual war I didn't recognize. I was a part of a traditional church where spiritual warfare tactics and strategic plans weren't a dominant factor in our time. I came from an era of the "prayer, scripture, sing your song, testify and tell all your business tradition." Come on. Stop, think, that's where you came from too. If someone didn't sing and testify or in some cases test-a-lie so they could feel like they've left a mark in the minds of people, they'd "Think of the goodness of Jesus and all he's done for them, their souls cried out Hallelujah (as long and as hard as they could hold it)." Oh yes, don't forget until it made the mothers of the church whoop and the young people shout for twenty minutes and then they would testify anyway, which only left the next saint a command of "Let no other stand, remember your sister or brother and now give a note of praise." This is how it was for me and I still say, "Give me that old time religion, its good enough for me."

In the meantime, recruiters for the United States Army were pulling me into the army of the Lord. I preached my first sermon on June 6, 1991, just after my high school graduation. "Trouble in My Way, Jesus Will Fix It After a While." I was seventeen and on fire for the Lord. There was a full choir stand and my godfather and bishop introduced me and my other godfather at the end did altar call. Some people came up for prayer including members of my family. I really felt that Jesus came in and anointed this service. Not I but the Christ that is in me. I always pray, "Lord, not my will but thy will be done." I've been so guilty of saying that down through the years, and it seemed as though the more I tried, the harder it got to live up to that. The devil gets no glory. But then I met a young man by the name of Westen. Westen was a sweet guy who was a preacher's kid I wound up losing my virginity with him at the age of 17½ upon my return from basic training and Army Individual Training. Westen and I met at Wars High School in Southport, Connecticut. I was running track. He picked me up and put me in the sunroof of his dad's Cadillac and said, "I just want to buy you an ice cream cone."

My next-door neighbor Jim told me, "He's okay, he's a great guy."

I said, "Jim, help me, don't let this 6'3" dude do me like this."

He was very honorable. He later said, "I knew you wouldn't come otherwise, but I like what I see."

So days turned into one year and a half that we dated. I left for the military during that time as well as wound up getting pregnant. I wasn't going to keep the child. Then the Lord spoke to me, "Only the Lord giveth, and the Lord taketh away and blessed be my name. I have a work for you to do and you can do it successfully only if I show you first that I deliver and unless I put you in a place of deliverance; it is impossible for your life to be a testimony to women who will need to hear your message and testimony later."

So I made up in my mind that no matter what comes, I will raise my child and go on through pain, persecution, scorn, tribulation, and seclusion. I have always in some instances been on my on aisle of Patmos. However, I wasn't always out there for the word of God and testimonies of Jesus Christ. But I was just thrown out there, sometimes just to be left to die. But you know God said, like he told Elijah, "Go ahead under your on symbol of a Juniper tree, get rest, eat and rise up after you come to your senses. My strength is made perfect in your weakness. Come on child, dust yourself off, get up and start again."

So I did. I didn't wait until I was showing in full bloom of pregnancy to go to my pastor to let him know that I was indeed with child. It hurt him, but he said, "Daughter, I admire you for the respect of telling me and I respected God enough not to pretend that nothing's going on. Nevertheless you have come to ask, what is my punishment?"

I had to sit out for a complete year. But I came to church, made every Bible class, every teen meeting, usher, choir, missionary board and Sunday school class and of course Sunday services. I yet recognized God forgives and that if you bear no cross, you surely will have no crown.

I had my beautiful princess. She was brought up in holiness and she received the Holy Ghost at the age of nine years old. This was long after Westen had disappeared and denied my daughter after her birth for ten months. Then I saw Jaquis again. This time, we hit it off really well. By this time, I had invited him to the wedding of Marvin and me. I changed the location at the last minute so therefore he couldn't come and stop it. In my heart, I was hoping he would have made a way to find out where it would be held. It would have stopped me in my mind for making a great mistake. But I didn't know God had predestined my life to go another way. Because he felt that I could handle all this, he moved his hand and allowed my will and not his will. Nevertheless, disobedience will teach patience and to wait on God. I had a great problem with patience. To be brutally honest, I still do. Even though God has allowed me to graduate from dimension to dimension, I'm learning every day how important it is to have God's stamp of approval on your life and to listen to the Chief Shepherd. For this, a sheep hears his master's voice and a stranger he will not follow.

I was married to Marvin, yet I was still lonely. We were on a different page in life altogether. Well, I already stated, "I came out of that!" with a mind to serve God. Then the divorce came and I met Jaquis again. This time, he and I finally visited his Dad's church and I was twenty-one. My daughter was five months old. I decided that if he asked me, I would be his girl. So we saw one another, talked like we did before, all night long. It was just like old times. Of course, we decided to give love a try. This jive time joker was seeing a young lady that was a lunatic musician and the other one he was breaking up with couldn't half read but she wanted to read me my rights concerning him. May the best woman win in a fight over any man. He will have you and this girl fighting over here and getting a phone number over there and not wanting either of you when it all boils down. So he got rid of all the counterfeits and he decided to step up to the real woman at the plate, me. So we discussed marriage, had counseling, and dated about one year.

One day, his van broke down and we took it to get fixed. This was his only means of transportation. I was walking around the van, and on one knee, he said, "Shawnta, will you marry me?"

said, "Get up, and stop playing with me!"

said, "I'm not playing."

Then, tears rolled down my face like Niagara Falls and I said, "Yes, yes, yes!"

"By the way, if all I had to do was get your raggedy van fixed, I could have been married."

We kissed, kissed, kissed, and oh yeah, did I mention we kissed again. We laughed and made plans later to get married. In preparation of our wedding for June 16, 1994, we wound up getting married on February 27, 1994. For no other reason than Uncle Sam was calling. I had orders to report to a Fort in Kansas so we pushed the date up as soon as possible. So in case of emergency or if anything happened to me, my daughter, my son, and my new husband could be taken care of. We got married as planned. His sister was always throwing a monkey wrench into everything. She asked him, "Why marry someone who doesn't want to have another child? Why marry someone who has to leave you? You know how military life can be."

I told him, "You're listening to her, and she hasn't served one day and still hasn't had one child. So until she has walked a mile in my shoes, she should just shut up!"

Well, he had no choice but to let me go. Although my natural father was not around, Uncle Sam had taken his place in the natural realm. I finished my tour of duty and came back a sergeant. So when I returned, I got asked all these crazy questions by Jaquis, "Did you really go to service? Did you really go for training and what was it about?"

I asked him, "Did you really drop me at the airport? Did you really see a recruiter there to make sure myself and eight other people boarded the plane? Did you kiss me goodbye as I gave them my ticket to board? Did you come or was it your reincarnate?" I told him, "Okay, by the way do you see any military police looking for me right now? So, babe, why would you ask me such a dumb question?"

He said, "Well, all the family seems to say you went to see other guys or something."

I said, "That's the trick of the enemy. They only gave our marriage six months to last so they are working overtime at it."

"Honey, let them worry about it," I said. "Now, how are the babies, and has my mom been taking good care of them?"

He said, "Of course."

I wound up having to leave again pretty soon to receive a double military occupational specialty (MOS) because we were strongly thinking about leaving Connecticut to get away from everyone and send money to help Rev. Hopewell build a new church. However, while I was in Fort Sam, Houston, Texas, I was receiving a new MOS and my wrist got broken. My daughter was home with pneumonia, and I was down to the end of completion when my wrist prevented me from continuing on. Then I had a family emergency to leave and go home. The chaplain, brigadier general, and company commander had to send me home due to my child. As I approached home when I exited the plane, my husband and I had the wedding due on June 6, 1994. This was because all of the dresses were made and we couldn't repay everyone. It really bothered me that his only sister wasn't in our wedding and we were so close at one point. We were the same zodiac sign (if I believed in them, but I don't). It seemed as though she had a problem with the fact that we married before she did. When she did get married, she and I were pregnant at the same time and

I had my baby first so she had a problem with that. Each time, I was pregnant with her and my child was first. I didn't care but she allowed the competitive spirit in her to rule over her, therefore making it very difficult for us to get along. Now, if that wasn't enough, she became heartlessly jealous of the Reverend's and I relationship. She told me, "You will never be his daughter."

I said, "But on the contrary, see this piece of paper that gave the Hopewell name. Well, sorry to inform you that by law, I'm a daughter-in-law, and by the blood in Jesus's name, I am a daughter."

Then, as the years passed, Mr. Hopewell, Dad as I called him, got really ill and kind of weak. So the members barbecued and had different services for the upkeep of the church. I even worked with him while I was pregnant. From basketball, volleyball, skating, electrical, and carpentry, whenever you saw Jaquis, you saw Shawnta. But we allowed Satan to start building a wedge in our house and relationship. His sister went to Arizona and talked to her other brothers about me simply because of jealousy mostly I think but mainly out of spite. She despised the fact, number one, we got married and, number two, all the church programs were prosperous. She and her mom got so mad one time that they made a statement to the good reverend that, "If she told you to go stand on the roof, you would do it."

His reply was, "Yes, I would and how can you argue if she tells you to do it and God brings whatever she says to pass and shows the fruit of her labor? Is that not wisdom? Be mindful that you all are trying to hinder a vessel of God." He shared with his wife, "If you try to do harmful and damnable things to someone else's child, remember you have children also. Remember, whatsoever a man sowed that shall he also reap. Shawnta has been good to us, she's been faithful to God, service, and this family." So he told his daughter, "If I were you, I would leave her alone. She's not a punk, she just believes in family."

So the years came and the years went. Jaquis and I had many ups and downs. It seemed liked the more I shared with them about all the bad things Marvin did to me, the more he did similar things like asking me for intercourse even before I was done with my six-week checkup. Like having rough sex until I had to soak in hot water. Let me not forget that when I said no, he would wait until I was asleep and have sex with me anyway. I felt so used and mistreated by certain family members. I worked and went to school six days a week to finally finish my Associates of Arts Degree so I could feel like I had finally accomplished my goals (with four kids and a husband). My husband had such a lustful spirit, he couldn't see past it. A great and dynamic woman of God who was also a pastor, a mother, and a counselor to me told him that's a spirit and you need deliverance.

So after so many times of feeling unwanted and always the secret center of conversation when his other brothers would come to town, I decided since other men were good listeners and since they didn't take advantage of me. I needed to feel love, respect, and wanted by someone, so I had several affairs. One affair I had felt like it would be forever. We did things we both enjoyed together. But the devil had me tricked to think that I would be able to live a life like that and be God's chosen vessel. Although when I left that relationship, another person pursued me. But I was feeling like if I can't please anyone in my family, then I'll find some joy in my sadness. It seemed like all the Hopewells were against me. I couldn't go to my own family because they would only laugh at me and say, "Oh, I thought everyone was so wonderful over there." So I stayed to myself. I never wanted to go to any family functions because no one wanted me there. Although no one knew about the affairs, I was now ready to give Jaquis what he had long been asking of me, a divorce. Mainly because I couldn't have sex every day two to three times a day. So one day, I decided this was the last straw when I came home and refused him, he would fight me and say, "You did it for other guys before me." One affair I stopped and the other I kept because I had felt a sense of security, sexiness, and I loved his charismatic way. But we all know in everyone's life, a little rain must fall. So we agreed we wouldn't see each other anymore. I wanted to start over and make things right with my husband the best I knew how.

We renewed our vows for the third time because we were trying to hold on to our marriage. So we went to Las Vegas for our anniversary and new honeymoon. We had a nice trip. Well, his biggest problem has always been the money. When we got a little low on money, the trip was over as far as he was concerned. I said, "But, sweetheart, we have enough to eat. We've done all we wanted to and we are leaving in another day and a half." So we visited our cousin Lavera and found our way to her house. As he would tell it, she saved the trip for us. Well, I say we got out of St. Louis for a real honeymoon finally and I tried to do a cruise with him but had a problem with that as well. We never went on the cruise, and the honey still was dipped out of the moon!

Not long after the wedding, I had a hernia surgery, and then later a hysterectomy, we began to argue again. Now, he told me that I had a hysterectomy I could get up to do something. But I was put on bed rest. Even though I tried to do something. I had fourteen steps in my old home. I went to do some cleaning downstairs and I fell down the whole two flights and had to lay there until someone came home. My oldest son came. He helped me to slowly get up. My daughter placed a pillow under my head and called their dad to tell him. He talked to me. My son made me a sandwich, gave me some water, and made me comfortable for another thirty minutes until their dad came home. My son was placed on a two-week suspension during my recovery and he helped me fix my meals brought me water and everything.

He was only 8½ years old. He microwaved eggs, bacon, Salisbury steak, and vegetables. My kids were very independent. My daughter was 9 years old. She cleaned the house and helped me to the shower a lot. But it made me see that no one was there but my kids and me. When all the church members knew I was ill, family, and some friends, I leaned and depended on the Lord.

The only person that came to see about me was my husband's Aunt Milly. She would always come during my pregnancies and after my surgeries to assist me as much as she could. Then my Uncle Marcus and my Aunt Rachel would keep my two oldest kids when I had my third child. Upon the conception and delivery of my fourth child, Uncle Marqus and Aunt Rachel were there again, always willing to help me and assist me. Yes, I had to pay them sometimes but never could I pay them enough to keep four kids at maybe $40 a pop. They were good to Jaquis and me. We would go on anniversary outings and everything, but whenever we called, the two musketeers came to the rescue for us.

My life was spinning so fast. I was always being accused of something. It seemed that there was always a trap being laid for me. I then was accused of wanting my father-in-law, my brother-in-law, and it seemed to never end. But I tried to do as Jesus said, turn the other cheek. These scriptures kept coming to me. To obtain friends, you must first show yourself friendly. No weapon formed against you shall prosper. Just when I felt like giving up, I asked God, "Lord Jesus, can you hear me, can you see what's happening to me? Why me?"

He said, "If I have been tempted arm, yourself likewise. Fret not thyself because of evil doers and be not thou envious of the workers of iniquity for they shall soon be cast down and wither away as the green herb."

In the meantime, I'm saying to myself, "Yeah, Lord, but when? I want to see some consequences and repercussions now! I'm talking instant gratification."

All along, my great-grandma Salina would tell me, "Shawnta, you can make it. God is not allowing all this for nothing. It is the making of you. Great ministries have been birthed out of testimonies of deliverance. So go on, endure hardness as a good soldier, you will reap a harvest of blessing if you faint not."

But later, in two years, at the turn of spring, heaven sent angels down and gave Grandma her wings. She was a great woman of God who always tried to keep Jaquis and me on the right track. If she would have known that we were divorced, she would beat both of us down.

My husband never took a stand for me. He was always taking sides with his family against me. So one day, after our base had an early dismissal, I was talking to Ian. He was a road supervisor who liked me. But I didn't know until later on. I called my husband's sister to ask her when everyone was meeting at our in-laws' house so we could have couple's night at a movie. Then I hung up my cell phone. My cell phone accidentally called her back by the push of a button. Ian was asking me and another saved girl named Katrina would we like to ride with him to Long John Silvers because we had an early dismissal day and all the bus drivers would get together and take a bus to go and eat on early Fridays. So Ian knew I had a problem with a girl riding the bus and offered the two of us a ride. But in the process, he reached for his wallet and discovered he left his wallet at home. So he told us we could ride the bus to Long John Silvers but we could ride back with him. So we said, "Sure, okay."

Little did I know and to my surprise, my sister-in-law was eavesdropping. She took it all over the family that I was having an affair, but I really wasn't. She even lied to Reverend Hopewell and told him someone told her that I was seen coming out of his house. She really added it on. I caught my husband before she did and told him I'm not doing anything. Huh, blood is thicker than water and marriage in this family. Well, of course he believed her. Even after I told him that two weeks before that, she said she was going to do all she could to get me out of this family and she kept going even to the extent of lying to get it done. When I talked to her, she owned up after the damage was done. She said she heard the conversation on my telephone and that no one told her from my job. Then I also told her, "You also lied about seeing us at his house." I never knew anything about Ian. All I knew was that he was the safety supervisor for the bus company.

Then when Jaquis asked me again for the divorce, I told him, "Okay. I know you want someone else. Because what I won't do twenty times a day, seven days a week, I guess you feel someone else will. Right?"

He said, "Shawnta, tell me the truth. I can handle it."

So I told him the truth of the other affairs before but that I wasn't having one this time. I was innocent. But I learned the hard way, people say they can handle the truth, but in most cases, not the unadulterated, naked, brutal truth. So my advice is to only tell what you can handle because the price can be *very costly*.

I've always told the truth no matter what. The truth will make you free as long as you have another mature adult on the other end receiving those truths after they have requested the whole truth and nothing but the truth, so help them God. Because the realistic view is, some people are looking for a way out. Otherwise they couldn't leave on their own. Yes, that's called a coward. Don't throw rocks and hide your hands. Even through all of that, he still wanted his divorce, so I obliged him on March 17, 2003. Jaquis apparently thought that there was a bionic woman alive who was going to let him have sex with them all day and all night. Jaquis and I separated, dated other people, and tried to go on with our lives.

In the meantime, Ian stepped up to the plate with me. So everything that they thought looked true, but it wasn't true at all. Meanwhile, Ian was going to church and I was beginning to like him very much. I invited him over for dinner. Jaquis had long moved out and lived with his mom and dad. Then when I tried to explain to him, Ian was expendable. He didn't mean more than our marriage. I begged him on my knees to give us another try but he decided, "No!" He said and I'll never forget it, he declared, "I wouldn't marry you if you were the last woman on earth."

I said, "You are mad. You don't mean it."

He said, "Yes, I do, and if there is nothing else, I'm gone."

So I picked up the pieces of my broken heart. Then Ian and I started dating and Jaquis started coming over, saying, "What is he doing in my house?"

I kindly told him that this wasn't his house any longer. He had already filed for divorce, even after I begged him to start over again. But he told me that if I was the last woman on earth, we would never be together again. So I began to really like Ian. Then Ian and I set a date to be married about two months after my divorce. I felt so hurt and upset and I thought I would be able to pick up the pieces of my broken heart. I felt so rejected by a man I loved, enjoyed, and admired. I thought we were inseparable, but I was wrong. I still went to Jaquis. I told him, "Let's begin again. I don't have to marry this man. He and I together could never equal out to almost ten years of love, laughter, and late-night rendezvous."

Jaquis said, "Give us another chance!"

He said, "No, it's too late!"

So I decided the wedding is on and I won't turn back.

The next thing I heard was that Jaquis and Samantha, a girl he dated a long time ago, were going to get married. I talked to him in front of church on Sunday. I told him, "Don't make the same mistake I did. You still have an out."

But he told me, "I don't want to have sex out of wedlock."

I said, "Jaquis, second best isn't worth settling for and you should have your own house and be established so that you can't be put out again as you said to me. Please listen. God isn't pleased with my decision and he won't be pleased with yours either. Do you know why?"

He asked, "No, why?"

"Because we should still be together and you know it. Remember how we looked at each other after our court date? Remember what we felt. Everything felt so final, but we still honestly wanted to make love to one another." I told him he would always be the father of my kids and me the mother. "Jaquis, I feel we should always continue to be great friends for the children's sake if nothing else."

Jaquis agreed that nothing and no one would keep him from our kids. But if I had to start writing about that, they would give me a Pulitzer Prize for the Best Author merely because he allowed a wedge to come between me, him and our kids. A big wedge weighing in at about 165 lbs. and about 35 or 36 years old. Yep! You guessed right, his wife.

Jaquis really had to learn how to be a little more firm. He was always firm with me, but with her, it's like that commercial, "Uh, could you please pass the jelly." I was basically referring to his weak mentality. He has always been that way, except with me. I tried to make Jaquis keep his word and do what he said. I told him that a real man has his strength and his word. If you don't keep your word, you are almost useless and unreliable. But his sister would always feel like I was trying to wear the pants. But my husband asked for help in these areas. Otherwise when she needed him, he would not show up for her either, unless he'd say, "Babe, will you drive? I'm really too tired and I don't feel like doing anything."

I would always say to him "Jaquis, remember—"

He would cut me off and say, "I know, babe, it's bad for my business and I should keep my word."

But as I said, she was always so busy working overtime in my marriage until hers started to diminish. You first have to clean up the leaves in your own yard before you can begin to start on your brother's or sister's yard.

So when I returned from my honeymoon, guess who was parked on my front. Jaquis, with tears in his eyes. And for once, I heard the scripture, "The race isn't given to the swift, nor to the strong, but to the one who endures to the end." I knew I had made such a grave mistake in my life.

He just walked to the door and said, "I came to see the kids."

I said, "Sure go ahead." My heart burned all that week because when I went to bed, I saw his face, when I rose in the morning, I'd see it again. I would sit in the tranquility of my bubble bath crying and feeling heartbroken. I tried to get my mind off him. Not even sex with Ian; as a matter of fact, it made it worse. Well, when you change the course that God has destined for your life, you feel like it's just you against the world. But God has not forgotten you. Although you walk through fire, I've learned you shall not be burned. So fear not. God is with you until the end. Fear not. God will redeem you. He has called you by name. Fear not, God has not given you the spirit of fear, but of love and of power and of a sound mind (Isaiah 43:1–3, 7, and 10).

So many times as I went through my heartaches and my pains. Even though my husband made me feel like what I wouldn't do someone else would, I kept my head up and I reached down in my soul and always provoked a praise.

There was always the word. And many times I had to reach in my sanctified soul just to find that song that ministers to my situation. At that time it was, "When peace like a river attended my way, when sorrow like sea billows roll. Whatever my lot thou has taught me to say, it is well, it is well with my soul." Then there were times in my life during this time, I said, "Lord, when and how much can I take. If it be thy will, take my cup from me."

Jesus spoke to me and said, "Remember a good name is rather to be chosen than great riches and after all thy disobedience I shall reestablish and then change your name. Your name will be a name of honor again."

I said, "Yes, Lord. Although you slay me, yet will I trust you! Some trust in chariots, some in horses, but we will remember the name of our Lord God. Some know not in whom they believe but I will believe in the Lord."

I had to encourage myself because I had a very few people encouraging me. There were more trying to hinder me. It seemed as thou no matter what man I dealt with, no matter what hurts, what truths, what untruths came out, I had to bar the blame and took the shame. While the men were yet honored, yet went on in the Lord, yet another notch in their belts, another statue in their Curio Hall of

Dames, and a handshake from their friends, a chip off the old block statement from their dads, while I suffered to be called a whore.

I decided that this wasn't my name but that I am what God says I am. The best part in all this is, I knew I was coming out of this too. Come run with me to chapter 2 because I'm coming out of this "with my hands lifted up and my mouth filled with praise, I will bless thee oh Lord!

Why Beat Me to Keep Me

"Good night, everyone! Bye! See you all tomorrow," I said as I left my job as a nurse's assistant at the Riverview Nursing Facility. I usually worked an 11:00 p.m. to 7:00 a.m. shift just so I didn't have to sleep with Marvin, my husband. So I was on a 3:00 p.m. to 11:00 p.m. shift this particular night.

On my way home, I stopped just before I would go into my apartment and say to myself, "Okay, be jolly and comply with him and he will do his thing and go to sleep."

I turned the key and I asked him, "How was your day?"

He responded, "A day, yours?"

I said, "It's okay. Honey, did you get my note that I said don't use the tub for twenty-four hours because the maintenance man sealed and caulked the tub?"

Marvin said, "Woman, you don't tell me what I can and cannot do in my own house, you understand! Now I got your note, but I used the tub anyway."

I said, "Marvin, I'm not trying to tell you what to do. However, the water is running down into the Williams' apartment and I'm not able to pay for his apartment repairs because we didn't follow the rules of the landlord."

"Shawnta, let me tell you one thing, I do as I well please. Do you understand that?" He was taking everything out of proportion.

I said, "Okay. Just forget it."

"No, let's not! What are you doing home so early today? I thought you worked 11:00 p.m. to 7:00 a.m.?"

"Yes," I said, "I took and earlier shift to switch with someone else for another day."

"Well, come on. Get it ready, I want some."

I told Marvin, "You know I'm really tired and sleepy. I had heavy patients to lift today."

Then he said, "Okay," and slapped my face and got on top of me and said, "I said it's time and you're gonna have sex whether you like it or not."

I cried as he ripped my panties off and proceeded to have sex with me roughly and painfully even to the point of bruising me. So as he raised up off me I gathered myself as in a drunken stupor to the bathroom to soak in Epsom salt and hot water.

Tears running down my face as the flashbacks came across my tormented mind. Flashbacks of him busting open my stitches after having my oldest and only daughter. Only after being out of the hospital 3½ weeks. He told me, "I'm not waiting for a six-week checkup. I'm gonna make sure you're checked up in my way and I will help you heal when I apply some protein."

But as I sat in the tub, rocking back and forth, the Lord brought to my mind, "My child, remember, no weapon formed against you shall prosper."

Then, I began to scream in silence and he said, "Shawnta, how was that? What's my name? I'm still *big daddy*, right?"

I gathered up all my tears and hurt and let out a fake, "Yes! You're still the man."

Although hurting inside and out, not really knowing whether to kill him or myself. I heard the Lord say, "And, lo, I am with you always, even unto the end of the world. I shall fight for you. Be strong in the Lord, and in the power of his might."

I got out of the tub that night and I prayed, "Dear God of heaven, Jesus, deliver me from this man and, Lord, forgive me for going contrary to your word and to your way. Lord, if you give me a way out and a scapegoat, Lord, I will leave and never look back." I came out of the bathroom and went into the living room. I began to cry out to God softly and I asked God for strength to go through until he brings me up and out.

So I fell asleep on the couch, and the next morning, Marvin got up for work at McDonald's and I saw him to the door and gave him a peck goodbye. But as usual, he said, "Baby, I'm sorry. You know I love you and will do anything for you and the baby." Then, I felt so numb to those words because they meant nothing after the third, fourth, fifth, sixth, seventh, and eighth time. I could go on with numerous apologies but always broken promises of I'll never hit you, rape you, or hurt you again.

However, later that afternoon at 2:45, Marvin came in and he had been stumbling pretty badly. He said, "I'm so tired, I'm going to lie down."

So I said, "Okay, fine." I took his clothes off him to get him ready for bed. I found a clean plastic wrap in his pocket with a white rock in it and a small antenna cut off at both ends. I put it back in his pocket and went back to sleep for work later that night, I left and went to work with what I found on my mind. I never knew he was using drugs and drinking too. I hung my head low, feeling what I have done to deserve all this. He was baptized, he was trying to receive the Holy Ghost. But even so, he wasn't strong enough to say no to drugs, mental and physical abuse. He could always tell me no and what I could and cannot do, regardless to what I wanted or my ambitions.

Well, here I am on my way home. It's now 7:30 a.m. My night of work is done. I go to our ladies room, freshen up a bit, and pull out some fitting black lace undies, bra, and stockings. Then I slipped back into my nursing white uniform once again. I told myself, "Get ready, Shawnta, and pump yourself up. Get ready for this. Remember, you are only here for a season now enjoy it." So I convinced myself that this is the man I fell in love with and I'm going to give it one more try. I turned the key and said, "Marvin, come on. Let's get it on while I'm in the mood." I also made up in my mind that if he put his hands on me again tonight that I was not going down anymore. I shook myself and I began to gain some courage. I said, "I shall live and not die. I refuse to die inside while he remains fine and controlling." This is the day I told myself. This day he's either going to do what I say or leave me alone. Little did he know, I checked into Job Corps to see if I could go there once I decide to run. I also thought about whose house I will run to. How will I get out of his clutches?

When I came into the bedroom, I told him, "Baby (real smooth like), why don't you shower and I'll slip into something a little more sexy and inviting."

He said, "All right! That's what I'm talking about. You get ready. I'll take my shower." Then, real quickly I went to the kitchen and slid four knives under the couch (two on each side) and he came out of the bathroom. It started to rain and hail real hard outside. We had a balcony at that time. I unlocked the balcony door for easy outage for him. He then wanted to put something new into the game. So he pushed me down on the couch and began to rip my panties down and off. I said, "Marvin, stop! Stop! Please! Oh, God! Help me! Don't Marvin!"

He replied, "Girl, lay down."

I said, "Let me, let me adjust myself."

"Okay, Okay!"

Then my left hand went into the side of the couch and my right hand in the back crack of the couch. I was then lying on my stomach. I cried, "Marvin, let me up first." He had on shorts and no shirt. I rose up on all fours and said, "Come on. Okay, scoot back some." Then I jumped up on my feet and jumped on the floor, cornered him by the sliding doors, swinging the knives like I'd lost it. But I had full control of what I was doing.

He jumped up and said, "Woman, are you crazy? What's wrong with you?"

I told him, "Slide the door and get out!"

He said, "Okay, calm down."

I kept swinging like I was going to stab him. I just wanted him on the balcony and out of my way. It was raining and golf ball-sized hail and cable wires, telephone wires, and electrical wires were up by our apartment. I locked him out, got all the clothes I could, and took my car and left. He was hollering, the security guard came and I told him what had happened. The security guard said, "Shawnta, get all your stuff, I'll talk to him and get out of here," and he used the words, "And don't come back!" Security had come on numerous occasions to my apartment through black eyes, bruised thighs and arms. He asked me, "How long, Shawnta? How long will you stay?"

I would just say, "I'm coming out of this. I've got to plan my time." But when I do, I won't look back. Holding my busted lip. Barely able to talk. He told Marvin to be quiet or he was going to report the altercation to the office, and he would be put out.

So with my daughter in her punkin' seat and all my clothes in the car, I left him and that life and pursued happiness. I applied for a divorce, actually an annulment because it wasn't long. But it was a divorce because it was consummated. I drove to my Aunt Ann's house to have time to register in Job Corps. My mom watched my daughter so I could go to school and I fit in quickly because I saw my dearest friend there as well. I remembered Renita told me about this place so I tried it. Then, I enrolled, and to my surprise, I found out I was pregnant. I hated Marvin for that because he always tried to hold me back in life. So I thought seriously about giving the baby up for adoption. I didn't need another child. So when I was 7½ months pregnant, Job Corps expressed to me that I had to leave because they couldn't be responsible for me and my child.

Just as I was leaving on a weekend pass, I went to my daughter's grandparent's home to do laundry. I left my car unlocked as I was loading my clothes back into the car. I went to put the bag in the front seat and I sat in the driver's seat. Up from behind my seat, a 6'1" Marvin was stooped down behind my seat. He had followed me that evening. Somehow, he had knowledge that I was just leaving base. He drug me into the alley, hit my head on a concrete wall because it was his birthday and I didn't spend it with him. He busted my head and had sex with me in that alley. I was screaming and hollering, he kept on ramming and hitting me. My daughter's grandpa said, "Hey, get off her and let her go."

I didn't hear from Marvin again until one day I had to apply for welfare and have DNA done because DFS required blood test for child support. Marvin tried to deny that my eldest son was his child. But he forgot he busted my stitches after my firstborn child. His family found me and told me that he was in the hospital with cancer. My divorce wasn't yet final. I went to the hospital and gave permission for surgery. He had prostate cancer from an injury years ago that he didn't get checked out. So drugs and everything took its course in his body. It started with a bleeding ulcer and it evolved from there and spread throughout his body. I, the good wife, still went to see him in the hospital and took his baby boy to see him although he didn't know who his daddy was. He was too young to know him. The hospital took the swab of DNA blood work from him three days before he passed away. It was court ordered. He denied my son and the report came back 99.9% positive. He didn't want me to prosper. He wanted me to suffer at everything. The devil meant it for bad, but God meant it for my good.

I went to the funeral five days late. But a spirit of peace came over me when I knew I did all I could to be good to him, even unto his death. The divorce was final before his death. But God said, "I will fight for you and no weapon formed against you shall prosper." Although Marvin tried to hurt me, despise my son, and deny the truth along with his family, God still had my back in it all. So I say to you walk with me to chapter 3 'cause I'm coming out of this.

I've Seen This Test Before
Without an Answer Key

It was a sunny Friday and early dismissal for the bus company. Ian heard I was going through a divorce with Jaquis. This was right up his alley because he told me that he has always admired me. I said, "Really, how long did it take you to think up that line?" Then Ian asked for my telephone number, and after we talked about two to four weeks, we decided to go to dinner. He said to me, "I only take a woman who is special to me out to my favorite restaurant."

We pulled up to Red Lobster, and I said, "Okay! I really like seafood. It's one of my favorite dishes." I've been out to more expensive and extravagant restaurant than this. I would figure that a fifty-six-year-old man would take me somewhere like Sandals Resort in Jamaica or something. Not Ian, only Red Lobster. Well, I guess it was more about his conversation and not what we were eating at the time.

This conversation that Ian and I had was very inviting. He told me at a very vulnerable time in my life, "You know I'm really attracted to your charisma and your beauty." But honestly, as I thought closely about it, he was only interested in my collateral and my booty.

Ian was supposed to be saved, sanctified, and filled with the precious gift of the Holy Ghost and did speak in tongues as the Spirit of God gave him utterance. "Yes, right there you should be breaking a dance. Because he that findeth a Holy man findeth a rare thing." However, I was blind and almost refused to see that he wanted a good wife and woman. Nevertheless, he still had a habit he couldn't give up. I never knew that Ian smoked, drank alcohol, and later, I found out from various sources he was still using drugs. Ian's grandmother left her house to him before I met him and he told me that he lost the house due to an ex-wife and due to his feelings of not wanting to return from Las Vegas to come back to Connecticut. Ian really laid the icing on my butter-me-up cake pretty thick. In some things, I was naïve, in other things, I was just plain stupid. I must be real and open because it is very important that when God reveals, uncovers, and shines his light on a situation all hidden points of the situation are gone. I strongly believe that although God was trying to tell me something, I wanted companionship so badly after being rejected by Jaquis, I couldn't fathom being alone.

Just when I realized that I was already married to Ian, living a life of greatness, then Jaquis came over to our old house the day we got back from our honeymoon. He had tears swelling in his eyes and he looked at me and shook his head, and I began to have tears swell in my eyes for the first time in my life I really felt like I had made a heart-breaking, life-shaking mistake. My heart dropped and my spirit stood still. In the moment of stillness, our eyes met while Ian was in the house and I whispered to Jaquis, "I will always love you and I'm so sorry. I've assisted in us both hurting each other." Then the kids came out and hollered, "Daddy!" I went in the house and looked from the window as the Lord said to me, "You must learn patience, my child. You moved too fast." Then I really began to cry and grieve in my heart. God allowed me this time. In all that time. He allowed me to see, "This marriage is not my will, but since you wanted it, I allowed it to be."

Ian and I talked later that night. He pretended that night to be excited. However, he had forgotten that he stayed gone two days, never showed up to his bachelor party, and didn't show up until time for us to start moving things to the church for the wedding. We talked before-hand and he told me he was just scared and I told him okay. He said to me, "Sweet, what if I don't want it and I think maybe it's too soon for us?"

I told him, "I had paid too much for a dress, invita-tions, people, food, and everything. You had better pull it together, Ian. You will not leave me the embarrassment of being left at the altar." So only when he didn't show up until the last minute of the wedding did I realize this wasn't written in God's marriage book in heaven.

Ian and I went home to live together. The story was short lived because it really had a false since of life in it. It wasn't real love, but it was fabricated fallacies of love. He would get paid on Thursdays and the kids and I wouldn't see him again until Sunday, broke and broke down from the rendezvous over the past four days. I thought it was me. He always tried to make it seem like it was my fault one way or the other. Ian said, "Well, you're not here in the evenings."

However, in the beginning, everything was discussed about finishing listing for school and our ministerial class, "It's all about the Souls." I asked him in the beginning. Say right there to yourself, "In the beginning," because as long as love is covering a multitude of faults and disagreements, in the beginning everything is always all right. There were a lot of days spent alone for two months.

I was only Ian's wife for sixteen days and I graduated from a prominent Junior College in Connecticut. Ian decided he was not coming down to the Mayfair Grand Opera House to see his own wife graduate. He was only two persons to come out of three tickets I had was my daughter and my former pastor of the Jehovah Shammah Church and no Ian to show his face at all. As I got ready to leave, I saw my pastor. He said, "Shawnta, where's Ian?" I had to lie and tell him he was working. I felt so low when the man that performed our wedding ceremony was asking about my new sixteen-day old husband and I had to lie to keep.

Now it was even more shameful to find out he was doing drugs. I don't have what is called street knowledge so that's why I am a little slow to grasp some things. My grandma and my great-grandma kept me from street life as best they could. Even today, I can attest that the street never got a hold of me in all of this. I'm still here! I've never had a sense of turning my back totally on God. I made mistakes, but I always stayed around the saints because I knew

God himself was dealing with me ever since I was a child. Ian and I split up after two months of marriage. Then I lost my house, my van, and my cars. Ian would always mess up his money and I already had filed bankruptcy while I was with Jaquis. So he would never contribute because he would always come home with an "I'm broke" story. We moved from the south part of Connecticut to the north side where, in spite of my short comings, God blessed me with a ten-room apartment, which the total includes two full baths.

Well, I decided since Ian kept calling, asking can we try it again, we began to do so. So I moved in August of 2003. We gave it another real good try in view. However, it wasn't meant to be. Ian started all over again. But what I found out was Ian always blamed the women in his life for his shortcomings. He never saw that he had a serious problem. He was a retired cop trying to relive some old cop ways. Ian could cook, clean, and handle himself intimately to be an "old man" as we would call it. Most of all, he really showed favoritism with my children openly. He only wanted to cater to his favorite one of the four. But my hat goes off to him with respect for even marrying me and taking some time out with my kids. I shall always remember his faithfulness to football practices with my two oldest boys. He would have them there on time because he was really a man of timeliness. He believed in God, but I believe he was so down in despair because of the hand he felt he was dealt in life; so much so he want to church, had a form of godliness, and denied the power thereof.

So I went to church on a Sunday afternoon, to a visiting church to sing. And the word of the Lord came to me from a prophet saying, "The husband that you have now, he is not yours. He is going to be moved." So that Monday morning, the kids and I were upstairs preparing for school.

Suddenly, Ian comes in and says, "Sweet, I want to talk to you."

I said, "Just a minute, as soon as I'm finished with the kids."

He said, "Okay." Then he turned as if to go downstairs and, right in front of them, said, "I don't want this anymore."

I pretended to be saddened, but I said, "Lord, is this happening this quickly." Then he left shortly after and started moving that weekend to his sister's house. This was in early October. So then, as time went on, we still talked about our situation. He confessed to me he loved me, but it couldn't go on this way with us. I agreed. Although my heart was hurting and the devil was saying, "This is your third marriage and you've failed again. You might as well get someone to have sex with, live with, and be happy that way because everybody else is doing it." It's become known as the American way. Rebuking the adversary and telling him, "God promised me peace and he promised me prophecy would come to pass. So, Satan, I bind you and the thought of shacking. Yes, Lord, I've made some bad choices. But if you be my help, no weapon formed against me shall prosper."

I never had a thought of shacking up ever again until about one year ago when I felt that someone cared for me. Ian had moved with his sister and all was well with that situation until he would come out short on what was to be paid to her. One night, he called, asking can he spend the night because he and Samantha had gotten into a fight. I told him yes. After all I said, he's still my husband. Later, I thought while he's here, I might as well take advantage of having sex with him just to hold me over. If he asks me, I'm going to slip into something more seductive and not comfortable just in case of a second thought. So we made love.

All the while it was a part of making his move to come back. I told him, "Fine, a couple of weeks, until everything cools off." We planned Thanksgiving together and I was to be in surgery on the eighteenth of November. Well, my children were set to go to Indianapolis with their grandparents, Reverend and Sister Hopewell. Ian and I decided we would have Thanksgiving together. One day while he went back home to his sister's house, my eldest son and I went to the circus. No one was home but the two of us, and I decided on the sixteenth, before I have surgery, I would take him to the mall and asked Ian to accompany us. Well, as I was going down W. Florissant, Ian was passing by. He decided to go because he had told me earlier that his mom needed him for grocery shopping. Nonetheless, he lied again.

Capturing his eye, I blew the horn at him, he pulled over on a side street and I asked him would he like to go with us. "Oh, by the way did you help your mom with the groceries?" He was about to lie again. I said, "Never mind. You've always said you wanted a good wife. But I must ask you, can anything good come out of Egypt (Ian)?" I said, "Just give me my gospel CDs out of your company car."

So he let me get them as he walks away for a minute. So I got my things and got out. I guess he felt like I had something else of his and he ran back toward me and I ran toward my car and said, "What is it, Ian?"

He said, "You got my CDs as well."

I said, "Look, Ian, I don't. Here they are right here. These are all mine."

But he was trying to hit me while I was in my car because he was caught high and he lied. My foot accelerated 10 mph on the gas trying to leave, but Ian continued to hold on to my car. I then told my son, "It's all right, baby."

Ian still tried to hit me again in my face, so I pulled off a little faster. Since he wouldn't let go, he ran alongside the car and tripped, slipped, fell, and skinned his knee like a small strawberry because he was so fair skinned.

So my son and I went to the circus, came home, and a call came through. This call was from Ian's ex-girlfriend, Fontaine. Samantha had given Fontaine my phone number and they decided to call me and threaten to bust out all my windows in my apartment. Well, at that time, a very prominent alderman owned my building. So I tried to return the call. My caller ID wasn't working at the time so I used *69. Well, I called and asked to speak to Samantha, and Fontaine picked up cursing, saying, "Mother—Samantha isn't here B—just take Ian's stuff to Samantha's house." So I had to think were they coming. I don't know this woman and I'm told she's a drunk. So I gathered all Ian's things and took them out to Samantha's house.

Well, the door was open and they were exchanging the grandchildren. It was about nine people in the house when I knocked and was told just to come in. When I came in, everyone said, "Hey, Shawnta, how are you doing?"

I said, "Fine." I asked for Ian's sister so that I might give all his work, walkie-talkie, digital camera, badge, and

Nextel two way to him. She was in the back room and her daughter called her and said, "Mama, Shawnta's here for you."

When Fontaine heard my name, she came up out of their den saying, "What's up? Come on with it B—! You gonna' try to run my man over."

So I immediately looked for some items on their table and kitchen bar because they weren't far from each other. I proceeded to tell her as she was coming around the dining room table to try to fight me, "It's not going down like this." So I picked up their hammer and their knife to protect myself. Because remember my wrist was still considered fractured and I was due in surgery on November 18, that Monday. So Samantha comes out while grabbing my neck and Ian took the items out of my hand. She pushed me out of the house. I told my sister-in-law, "I can walk out."

She said, "No, I am throwing you out!" while everyone looked on (even my own husband). So while I was backing up and trying to leave Samantha's daughter and two of her cousins chased me and I never knew where I was running to exactly because I had only been to my sister-in-law's house two times. I ran to a cul-de-sac and they couldn't catch me, so one of them threw a 24-ounce beer can at me. It rolled under the car. I grabbed it and one girl said, "Throw it."

I said, "No! You come closer I'll bust your head, they'll see about you and then I can leave."

They quickly visualized that and said, "Let's block her car." So I couldn't leave. In the meantime, I hear the cops. My husband was standing there the whole time, never telling them to stop or anything. He could have prevented it all.

The cops came and I said, "I'm glad to see you because these people are trying to assault me."

Well, he put the cuffs on me because the ex-girlfriend called the police and then one of the other girls brought the weapons out and said I brought them to do bodily harm. So one cop took me to jail and let me go on my own recognizance.

Then, on that Monday, I went to the hospital to have an outpatient surgery that turned into a two-day hospital stay. While I was healing, Ian came over to assist me. My mom came to the hospital to see me and be with me. Ian would tie my hair at night for me. My kids would help me cook when Ian was at work. Then after he felt I was well enough, he was out doing his thing again.

Although many people don't see it, I've always had the favor of God no matter where I've been. The songwriter said, "Lock me up, throw away the key, but I'll make it. Through hard trials, tribulation, persecution, Lord, I'll be faithful. Yes, it's been sink or swim, live or die, I'll make it and you can too, my sister or my brother."

CHAPTER 4

The Mack and the Money

As the story goes on, I met a man after my divorce while I was going through all of this turmoil in my life. I befriended McHenry because to me, he was strategically placed for that time and season in my life. He was the only one who came to see me while I was in work release. He brought me money. I really loved this man, but he in return could never love me back. Because I found out that he himself was hurting. Sometimes when people are hurting, they hurt other people unintentionally. He would always say I was a good person and I would be a good wife to him. But he hadn't healed himself and I believe that maybe we both were a buffer for one another and a pacifier for the pain in our lives.

McHenry was a sweet man with a sweet heart. But it was stained and cracked from leaving God for reasons I shall not reveal. I've always kept his life sacred, in return I put mine in the open to some people. Even so, I'm in the

I'M COMING OUT OF THIS   47

book. When the word says love them, not like them. But love them that despitefully use you. McHenry was sweet to all my children. I felt that he should not have listened to a lot of negative-talking friends of his. But within himself, he will always bear the truth that, "No one will ever treat me like you, Shawnta. You have hard shoes to fill." But even this test with him, God allowed me to pass it.

What I've learned in this as God was bringing me out of all these stages of my life is that I always tried to replace him with a man and God was trying to take me to a place of destiny a long time ago. My pastor D told me recently that "Little one," she said, "I tried to tell you this years ago, but you wouldn't hear me. You went on," as she would say, "laughing through it with no remorse."

I said, "Pastor, wasn't that there wasn't any remorse. I never wanted to be lonely."

She told me, "But however hard the test and trials have been, little one, you wear them well."

Pastor D may not know this, but I often think of the message "Recapture the Glory." This is what I want in every aspect of my life, that the glory of the Lord be revealed in my life, souls are delivered, made whole, and set free. Pastor D has been a shepherd, mother, and a walking word of life to me. So no longer do I feel like a castaway because she has preached to my soul and our congregation.

"Attention! I'm still alive!" So mount me so I can fly from where I am as a great psalmist put it. Mount me above the darkest cloud of my life, set me on a mountain of deliverance. Put my head on a pillow of praise and fly with me for I have come out of this. And may God deliver you too!

I haven't received any empathy for what has happened to me. As a threat to society yet humble before a mighty God, empowered to preach his word. Don't count me out yet because I'm coming out of this. Even though I'm having an Elijah moment in life and I have pain hanging over as a symbol of a Juniper tree, Jesus yet feeds me, lets me rest, and tells me, "Rise, there is yet work for you to do." Man may have closed many doors in my face, but God let me know that he is the Door. I'm walking in the valley low. Even then, what do I see along the way? I saw a lily in the valley. As I continue to cry out to God, He hears me. With many tears I have made my bed a place to swim in my deepest wilderness. Yet when I reach the top, he gives me a pillow of confidence. When life for me seems so grim, yet there's hope and I'm coming out of this. When my character is in question and my loyalty placed on trial, God promised those whom I've called I qualified and because I know his name I am justified. Now, I really understand when the song writer says, "Walk on, walk on, with hope in your heart and you'll never walk alone."

God has not given me a spirit of fear but of power, love, and of a sound mind.

Some days, I felt like I was going to lose my mind. A still small voice whispers to me and says if I have been tempted, arm yourself likewise. I'm coming out of this one day. No more will I be talked about as a statistic in a magazine, television, or on a legislative report. No longer will I sit questioning God what, when, and how long. No longer will the enemy say to me, "I'll torment you until you bow down and serve me. Do you know why? 'Cause I'm coming out of this."

Coming out because I'm not in despair. Coming out because Jesus told me I could cast on him all my cares. If I never teach in another classroom, never secure another hospital position as the head of security, never work helping the sick as a nurse's assistant, never drive a bus full of kids, never drive another limousine for another funeral home, or never get another degree, I'm coming out of this, you best believe. I'm more than a conqueror through Jesus Christ who loved me. My father, my mother, some of my family, friends, and men I thought that loved me have come and gone. I'm coming out of this because God promised me he would never leave me alone. I'll leave this with you in just phrase, "Mount me so I can fly from where I am. On the wings of an eagle, I'm coming out with my head lifted and my heart filled with praise and preaching a word of deliverance." I don't believe he brought me this far to leave me. I don't believe he brought me this far, gave me a Job testimony, and he spoke to my situations as though I was the Samaritan woman who had five husbands and the one I had at the time wasn't mine. But through it all, I'm coming out of this, knowing that God choses wisely because I have a destiny. I jumped off the road to glory to stop by way of my own story. I never realized that Destiny was derived from destined. I made it through and I believe God loves me.

Lord, come, Lord Jesus, help me. I'm coming out of this! Now, I can say between 2007 to 2009, I came out. I am still victorious today in 2019. God bless me with his chosen husband for my life, filled him with the Holy Ghost, and he loves me as Christ loved the church and gave himself for it. My husband said to me in the sweetest tone,

"I have found the one who my soul loves!" I have come out and my soul loves Jesus, bless his name!

Whatever you do after this, you must plan an escape. You have to save yourself and your children if you have them.

Come Out!

Steps to Take to Come Out Forever

1. Pray, find a confidant, comply with abuser.
2. Start to save money.
3. Never tell the children.
4. Find a safe place unknown.
5. Try to keep a job as an outlet.
6. When abuser leaves, run!
7. Run because you and your children's lives may depend on it!
8. Acquire restraint orders for you and your children.
9. File for legal separation/divorce if applicable.
10. Do not look back!

ABOUT THE AUTHOR

Evangelist Beverly Ann Smith-Glasper is a mother of four children, a grand-mother of four, and a loving wife. Evangelist Smith-Glasper is a playwright, a writer, psalmist, choir director, praise and worship leader, and author of this book. Evangelist Smith has been through many trials and tribulations and  circumstances in her life in which the devil had tried to make her feel that it was almost virtually impossible for her to come out as she stood several times at death's door. Evangelist Beverly Smith-Glasper is a faithful member of the Radiant Life in Christ Apostolic Church in St. Louis, Missouri, under the great leadership of Bishop Illona W. Dickson, pastor and founder. Through facing the expectations of holiness to be married and to be filled with the Holy Ghost and live a life that is pleasing unto God, Evangelist

Smith-Glasper tried to lead a life that was both pleasing and acceptable to God and the church. While trying to hold on to tradition, she was not realizing that although she was searching for God some of the men in her life we're looking to control and not to lead as Christ loved the church and gave himself for it which left Evangelist Smith-Glasper in a position of domestic violence and domestic altercations in her life and throughout her ministry. But today, Evangelist Beverly Smith-Glasper arrested every demonic and satanic force that came against her by the power and the presence of the Holy Ghost and is now living free from domestic violence and now married to a man that loves her as Christ has loved the church and gave himself for it.

CPSIA information can be obtained
at www.ICGtesting.com
Printed in the USA
LVHW032129281122
734174LV00004B/752